Grandma Moses

American Primitive

Anna Mary Robertson Moses.

GRANDMA MOSES

American Primitive

FORTY PAINTINGS WITH COMMENTS
BY GRANDMA MOSES · TOGETHER WITH
HER LIFE'S HISTORY
INTRODUCTION BY LOUIS BROMFIELD
EDITED BY OTTO KALLIR

Doubleday & Company, Inc.
Garden City, 1947 New York

Table of Contents

Grandma Moses
American Primitive

Introduction
by Louis Bromfield

ABOUT SIX OR SEVEN YEARS AGO I began hearing from friends living near Williamstown, Massachusetts, stories about a wonderful old woman who lived on a farm and painted pictures which she sold along with the jams and preserves she "put up" during the summer. She was, they said, prouder of her preserves than of her pictures and when she was asked the prices of her paintings she countered with a question "What size do you want?" The price depended on the size.

I would have suspected that the pictures were like the mediocrities exhibited at the average Middle Western County Fairs but for one fact: my friends said the pictures were remarkable and I respected their opinions because they had the background, the culture, the taste, and the understanding to know a real picture, a good picture, from a mediocrity or an affectation. They were not impressed by any artistic snobbery concerning "primitives" nor were they people to be entrapped by any nostalgic feeling for quaintness and the "good old days." They were buying Grandma Moses' pictures and had even ordered some in advance, priced at her insistence, according to size.

And then I saw my first "Grandma Moses" and I understood their enthusiasm. What struck me immediately about the picture, and indeed about all the other "early Grandma Moses" which I saw, was the decorative quality and a kind of design and composition that I found in the Persian and Moslem Indian paintings I had seen in the East. In the pictures of Grandma Moses there was less formality, less smoothness, less minute attention to details but there was in both the New England and the Indian pictures the same sense of space and "of the whole" and above all a sense of the painter's intimate feeling for children and animals and color and the delights which only those can know who share an intimate feeling for nature and have found for themselves a satisfactory relationship with the universe. As in the Indian pictures, each figure, animal or human, painted by Grandma Moses, was caught in an arrested moment of action . . . children skating, dogs running and barking, horses galloping and rearing. Clearly these were the pictures of someone who had loved and been loved and had borne children and lived close to animals and had had a busy, happy life. I knew, without ever seeing her, that Grandma Moses was a wise, shrewd, happy old lady and that she painted for her own pleasure because she loved life and color and felt the necessity of communication to others through the medium, first of all of color, her own sense of the richness of life. It was clear that never in all her life had she known a bored moment . . . Her small world, whether viewed from her bedroom window, or from the window of a bus driving along the road, was at once a cosy and limitless universe which contained the keys to the knowledge of good living and understanding.

In those earlier pictures she often painted crudely, but this defect could not stifle the overwhelming sense of her satisfaction in life and her adjustment to the immense scheme of creation itself.

It is one of the remarkable things about Grandma Moses that after beginning to paint seriously late in life, she has gone on steadily learning and improving.

In the beginning she had to find her own way. She had to learn the kind of composition which gave her pleasure and satisfaction. She had to learn how to achieve the effects of color which so delighted her. She had even to learn about the materials and the tools she used and which ones permitted her to realize to the greatest degree the feeling she had inside her. She learned that a base of lustrous white, carefully prepared by her own methods after much experimentation, gave her pictures luminosity and even brilliance. She had to learn painfully and slowly how to achieve the hazy, constantly changing beauty of the distant Vermont hills and skies which she conveys so skillfully in her pictures. In fact she had to learn, herself, without help or advice, how to become a painter. As a result she always paints like herself.

I confess that for me many of Grandma Moses' pictures have a philosophical and at times even a literary appeal. She knows what country life feels like, and she conveys to the beholder the joy that is in a running colt, the singing beauty of a blossoming peach tree, the soothing peace of a clear, running brook. She does not paint any of these things separately, for themselves, but in a pattern, each in its proper relation to all the others. It is a pattern filled with the satisfaction of those who understand that any farm is a small but complete fragment of the universe in which all the laws of Nature are constantly in play, affecting the lives, the philosophy, and the faith of those who inhabit it.

There have been and are today many technically skillful artists who paint farm scenes and rural landscapes, but nearly all of them simply paint "pictures" adroit and sophisticated perhaps in design and color but without that luminosity, enthusiasm, and understanding which one finds in Grandma Moses' pictures. Too many of them are flat in spirit, with the smell of the studio about them. They reveal little inwardness or real warmth. They are simply pictorial, revealing or interpreting little or nothing.

A good farmer looking at most of the farm pictures and landscapes painted in our time might say "a pretty picture" or "no farm ever looked like that" and move on to the next one. In front of a Grandma Moses he would stop and chuckle and smile and sigh, for in it he would find not only every detail painted with satisfaction and understanding, but he would know at once that Grandma Moses understood his whole small world with its glories and hard work and those quick, deep inarticulate gusts of emotion which sweep over him at the sight of a newly born calf or a blossoming pear tree or at the smell of deep, rich soil, freshly turned to the warm sun in spring. He would recognize that Grandma Moses understood these fundamental things which make the good husbandman a part of the earth and the fullness thereof and make him invulnerable to the petty miseries and misfortunes which complicate and torment the lives of city-dwellers.

The great and increasing popularity of Grandma Moses with the general public and the increasing interest and appreciation of her pictures by more critical groups has its roots also in the satisfaction of a special hunger which is steadily growing among all people in this Age of Aridity and Agitation. It is a hunger for something deeper, more spiritual, and more satisfactory than the materialist philosophies and political doctrines or even the art and writing born of the Industrial Revolution. In a world in which mechanical inventions and mass production have led man to worship the machine while it destroys his own higher capacities and makes a slave of him, the pictures of Grandma Moses give one a sense of the profound and fundamental goodness of small things, of the peace and confidence and satisfaction that comes of the adjusted and happy relationship of an individual to the whole of life, the universe and Eternity. The pictures of Grandma Moses are as far removed from the clash and monotony of a Detroit automobile factory as they are from the assembly line abstractions of the later Picasso or the decadent painting of the Sur-realists, both born of an industrial-mechanical age, one in approval of, one in revolt against, the materialism of a world which threatens to destroy itself or be destroyed by its very worship of automobiles and plumbing, of aeroplanes and atomic bombs.

In such a world the paintings of Grandma Moses provide a sense of peace and adjustment to the natural laws by which we must live or be destroyed. In Grandma Moses' world there is the same zest and understanding of the eternal importance of small things which one finds in the peasant pictures of Pieter Breughel. His pictures have the robustness and earthiness of a Flemish male. Those of Grandma Moses are infused

[12]

with the quality of a New England woman who had divided her life between two of the most beautiful parts of the world—the Shenandoah Valley and the hills of Vermont. But both Breughel and Grandma Moses tell you essentially the same thing—that every day life is good and amusing and filled with richness and variety and beauty, if you choose to find it.

At least that is what I find in a Grandma Moses picture, and I have seen the same satisfaction in the eyes of others standing before one of her paintings, studying the figures of a strutting Tom Turkey, or a rearing colt, or a blossoming tree, or a child skating on the ice of the clear little river she loves so well and paints so often.

Grandma Moses
American Primitive

THERE IS hardly a career in the history of modern painting comparable to that of Anna Mary Robertson Moses, better known as Grandma Moses. She passed her eighty-fifth birthday in the fall of 1945. Five years before nobody in the art world had ever heard her name, and eight years ago she herself was not aware of possessing an artistic gift that was to take the continent by storm. No wonder that legends are already beginning to form around her figure.

A woman of biblical age, living somewhere on a farm for which she has cared all her life, and around which all her interests are centered, who is virtually indifferent to the fame that has come to her so suddenly, and not in the least interested in the financial success of her pictures, Grandma Moses has begun to fascinate the imagination of a wide public. A flood of essays and "human interest" stories about her have been published in the magazines and newspapers of this country, and now that the war is over, Europe also is beginning to take notice of her. Museums and important private collections in the United States have bought her pictures and have placed them among the works of great painters.

This fact is all the more remarkable because the pictures of Grandma Moses are greatly at variance in artistic conception as well as spiritual content with what we are used to seeing today in contemporary art. They contain nothing that would seem "interesting" to a modern public. They have no connection with what we like to call "the artistic expression of our time"; they are in fact the very contrary of this art.

Grandma Moses is called a primitive painter. Each of her pictures denotes plainly that its author has had no art training whatsoever.

[15]

She tries to make her pictures look as natural as possible and goes so far, for instance, as to use "glitter" on her winter landscapes in order to make the snow more realistic. To a person who tried to dissuade her from this practice, she once said: "Have you never been in the country on a sunny winter's day? You would have seen how the sun shines on the snow and makes it sparkle all over. To me there is no winter landscape without the sparkle on the snow." But in spite of such naturalistic endeavors, the details are often drawn "wrong" or are clumsily represented. And yet, viewed as a whole, every picture painted by Grandma Moses is perfect in its own right and emanates sincerity and purity of purpose to such a high degree that you forget all its shortcomings. The simplicity of her rendering, the childlike way in which she seems to take no notice of technical difficulties, are so convincing that her pictures cast an unquestionable spell over their beholder.

Her work has now found general recognition. The great public loves it—but so do circles that are wont to be sharply critical in their art appreciation. The longing for a simplicity that we have lost—not in the field of art alone—the yearning for peace, for contact with nature, which is growing more and more remote, perhaps the nostalgia for a childhood in which everything seemed simple and uncomplicated: all this draws us toward the paintings of Grandma Moses. Perhaps these factors also explain why contemporary primitive art, whose oldest living representative she is, arouses such vivid and widespread interest today.

We have said that Grandma Moses is a primitive painter—but what is a "primitive painter"? The present essay is not the place for a basic disquisition on the subject, yet it is important to set down some characteristics of primitive painting, not only because of their relevance to the work of Grandma Moses but also because a good deal of confusion surrounds the subject today.

Webster defines the word primitive as follows: ". . . pertaining to the beginning or origin, or to the earliest ages or period; . . . characterized by a quality belonging to the original state of man . . . by simplicity, rudeness or the like."

The works of art produced in prehistoric times, certain paintings of the medieval period, the earliest specimens of artistic expression by children, are, of course, ready examples. Clearly, the conditions under which a primitive work of art can originate have nothing to do with a specific period in the history of mankind. They existed thousands of years ago and may arise equally well today. For primitive works of art have certain common characteristics regardless of the period of their origin. They appear crude and childlike; they have illustrative and decorative qualities; they stress flat pattern rather than depth, because the artist does not master the rules of perspective. They often reproduce events out of the artist's own life, or happenings he has heard about long ago, which have impressed him so strongly as to occupy his imagination for years. Events widely separated in time are sometimes shown side by side in the same picture. A primitive artist may attempt to tell the entire course of a story with all its details in a single painting. Primitive art strikes one as spontaneous and close to nature. An "instinctive" sense of color and composition makes up for the lack of technical ability.

It is important, however, not to confuse "primitive" with "self-taught" artists. During the last few years it has become customary to label as primitive not only those works corresponding to the definition but almost everything originating from the hands of self-taught painters. Those who use the word in this all-inclusive fashion take into account the matter of regular art-training only; for them the style is not important. Such a superficial view of the subject has had a "simplifying" effect, for it has created an extremely large group of so-called primitives. Actually it has coupled into a single category two entirely different conceptions. Primitive painters are almost certain to be self-taught.

But self-taught painters may express themselves in various styles. They are not bound to any special form—to any limitation of idea and content, as are primitive artists. The style of a talented self-taught painter need not differ from that of a "professional," whereas the character of a primitive work is always distinctly set apart from professional art. This does not in any way imply that primitive art is "inferior," or, as we sometimes hear, a mere by-path of art. Genuine primitive art is genuine art. A good primitive picture has all the fundamental qualities of a good "professional" picture. If the creative motive that inspired a work was honest, if the artist can formulate his idea and recreate it in the beholder, his work is true art, whether produced with the help of schooling or not.

*

The work of Grandma Moses to a rare degree lives up to what we expect in a primitive painting. She would not even know what was meant by art and studio courses. She has never been to a museum. The only artistic inspiration within her reach probably consisted of illustrated school books, Christmas cards, nineteenth-century color prints and illustrations in magazines. One cannot set a definite date for the beginning of Grandma Moses' artistic production because, almost without being aware of it, she had done some painting on and off throughout her life.

She tells us in her autobiography (pp. 37-45) how as a child she loved to draw pictures and color them with anything bright that served her purpose. The table on which she now keeps her artist's paraphernalia, an old-fashioned contraption with panels on four sides, is decorated all over with landscapes. Asked when she had done them, Grandma Moses replied: "Oh, not so long ago, about thirty years." At that time she was kept far too busy as a farm woman to give much time and attention to her artistic inclinations. In later years she began to make yarn pictures and the approval and success they met with among her friends may have prompted her to devote herself more thoroughly to regular painting.

Her first works strongly relied on the examples of art which she had seen in illustrated books: she began to copy them. But even at this

[18]

early stage she strove not to produce merely an imitation but to transform it into something of her own. For example, in a copy of an old Currier and Ives print, her coloring and the atmosphere she lends to the picture surpass the original. She has made something new out of it, has given her personal style to the old composition. And this style can be found in all her paintings. It is so striking that every one of them can be immediately recognized as her work.

Her paintings are typical of America, more especially of the country where the state of New York borders on Vermont. The Moses Farm is situated in the Hoosick Valley, a lovely countryside of rolling hills through which the Hoosick River winds its way, with the Green Mountains range silhouetted in the distance. This is the landscape she had known and loved for a lifetime and where, year in and year out, she has watched the passing seasons.

Yet none of her paintings is "done from nature." The idea of sitting out in the open with all one's painting equipment has never appealed to her. She considers it "very impractical." After coming in-doors from a ride in the neighborhood, from a little trip to visit some relatives, or simply from looking across the valley from the steps of her porch, she will sit down at her table and start a picture to record the impressions she has just received. Sometimes she goes far back to the land of her memories, to her early married years when she lived in Virginia. All these familiar landscapes, dear to her and part of her very being, form the setting for various events that have taken place in more or less remote times: memories of her own childhood; stories she heard when she was young (and which were old even then); tales about her forefathers who lived in this same Hoosick Valley; history and folklore. She transmutes into painting, songs she learned in her youth, and which she still knows by heart; for instance, "The Old Oaken Bucket."

She is careful not to omit a single detail: every person, flower, or tree mentioned in the song must appear in her painting. Observing her

[19]

work, one is immediately impressed by the way she lives with the picture in process. She will tell you what events have taken place in the houses she is about to paint, and how the two farms on her picture were once linked by the story of a romantic love. Her work is not "ready for delivery" before all the persons and all the flowers of the song have been put into it. The pleasure Grandma Moses takes in making a picture, the playful imagination which goes into the making of every little detail, can be felt in the completed work: it remains always fresh and fascinating, it never grows dull, no matter how often one looks at it.

While the range of Grandma Moses' artistic expression is limited, she masters that range thoroughly. Her drawing is by no means faultless, yet she compensates for this deficiency by a sure sense of color and by an unerring instinct. Whatever her subject may be—whether "Sugaring-Off," or "Washday," or "County Fair," or just "Sunday"—you always feel that it is *her* Sunday and *her* Washday. She has never succeeded in producing a picture that went beyond her well-known and familiar sphere. For each of her pictures represents some small part of her own life, and in painting it she means to communicate her experience to others.

Grandma Moses never intends to produce any special "artistic" effect. Everything must be as "true to life" as possible, because she feels that this is the way to make herself clearly understood. The world of her pictures is bright and serene. Everything always seems in perfect harmony; she will not consider disagreeable and troublesome subjects. She loves color and uses it to give her pictures an abundance of life, freshness, and radiance. She does not regard gloomy colors as the "right thing" for a painter. And the reaction her pictures produce proves her to be right.

As we have noted before, Grandma Moses' first "works" were small yarn pictures, mostly landscapes, very skillfully executed in bright colors and copied from illustrations. The same subjects were repeated later in her painting and it is interesting to note how quickly she adapted herself to the new technique of oil. The first painting we know of was a small landscape (with cows) that she had previously done in needle-work. The painting is still very uncertain and hazy. It did not seem to satisfy her, since she repeated this picture several times, and each new version shows progress. Her instinct was her surest guide. Then she began to copy various subjects from postcards and reproductions. For the most part these efforts are both uninteresting and uncharacteristic of her later work. Not until she undertook a subject that meant some-thing to her from personal experience—it was her first "Sugaring-Off"—did she come into her own. Two of her early "Sugaring-Off" pictures have been reproduced in this book. They exhibit all the characteristics of the artist's style and can be counted among her best works. Her style has not appreciably changed since "Sugaring-Off" was completed, but the average quality of her production is much higher today than it was five years ago. Whereas at first she tentatively tried her hand at subjects that were not within her reach, she has now found her way and goes straight ahead.

*

Grandma Moses' first one-man show took place in New York at the Galerie St. Etienne in October 1940. It was an immediate success, although the exhibition included many of her early attempts in which her great talent was scarcely recognizable. The public and the press reacted with generous sympathy toward the newcomer. Soon after the exhibition closed, Gimbel's department store in New York City displayed the same pictures again and invited the artist to attend the opening. Grandma Moses accepted the invitation. It was the first time in thirty years that she had been to New York. Great changes had taken place since her last visit: the city itself and its bustling life seemed completely strange and bewildering. The old lady did not quite know what to make of it. Her exhibition had been arranged in a huge hall—the pictures were almost lost on the walls. Hundreds of people had thronged to the opening: the personal appearance of the old farm woman who had become famous overnight had been widely publicized by the newspapers.

When Grandma Moses entered the hall, she was led to a microphone in front of which she was to be interviewed. The old lady became confused. She looked tremulously at the crowd, composed largely of women. Whatever could they want? What was she supposed to tell them?—And so, after the speaker had introduced her, she decided to talk about the only thing which she felt could be of any interest to this public: her preserves. She told them how she made them, how good they were, and she produced a few small jars out of her handbag and offered them as samples. Attempts to bring her around to the subject of painting failed. Wasn't the way she painted her own private affair? It was something she neither could nor would speak about.

Later she described her visit to New York in these words: "Oh, it was shake hands, shake, shake, shake—and I wouldn't even know the people now. My, my, it was rush here, rush there, rush every other place —but I suppose I shouldn't say that, because those people did go to so much bother to make my visit pleasant." The city oppressed her; she declared she never wanted to come to New York again.

Sometime later she painted a picture to express her feelings: "Grandma Goes to the City." One can see her farm on the right. Two old-fashioned vehicles have just left the front door and are driving down the road. They are depicted in a style of bygone days, to stress the difference between past and present. The countryside around the farm fills the rest of the picture. Only far in the background, close to the left edge of the picture, can you notice the vision of a city with white houses. There are dark clouds all around, but the farm is bathed in clear sunshine. . . .*

During the years that followed her first New York exhibition,

* The picture, reproduced in this book, is a later version of this subject, in which an old automobile has been substituted for the carriages.

Grandma Moses painted a large number of pictures. In the autumn of 1942 she had her second one-man show in New York, at the American-British Art Center. Here the tremendous progress she had made since her first appearance in the art world could be plainly recognized. There was no longer any doubt as to her extraordinary talent. Her style had grown more assured, the coloring more discreet. She now handled delicate shades and hues with a mastery which her early works had never achieved. The outlines had grown softer, and she reached astonishing effects of depth and space.

The most striking picture of the exhibition was "Black Horses." It shows a light green, hilly landscape with mountains in the background. The different shades of green in the meadows and fields are wonderfully brought out. In order to give depth to the picture, the artist framed the landscape with trees on both sides, a group of birches to the left and a single tree to the right, like a stage setting. The trees grow out of a narrow strip of land in the foreground, which enhances the impression of looking into a wide green valley. The black horses are seen cantering around the tree at the right. As with some of her figures, the drawing is faulty and awkward, and yet those horses focus the attention so strongly upon themselves that one takes them for the main object of the painting, and the landscape becomes a mere setting—a foil for the two black horses. You could almost call the composition of this picture sophisticated, if it did not, at the same time, impress you as utterly naïve and simple. There is nothing unnatural or studied about it.

The instinctive mastery of coloring and composition, as found for the first time in "Black Horses," comes to light in subsequent pictures. The works of this period are among her best and most popular. To name but a few: "The Old Oaken Bucket," "Over the River to Grandma's House", new versions of the "Sugaring-Off" and "Catching the Turkey" themes; views of Hoosick Falls; and the "Checkered House," which brought her as an exhibitor to the Metropolitan Museum of Art in New

York when that painting was one of the hundred-and-fifty pictures selected among a competition of five thousand to form the "Portrait of America" show. All these pictures have been reproduced innumerable times, helping to spread the name of Grandma Moses throughout America.

Soon she began to receive fan mail from all over the country. People who had seen reproductions of her works wrote to ask whether she would not paint them again for them. Eager to please everybody, Grandma Moses accepted "orders" of this kind. She regarded all those who wanted her pictures as her friends whom she could not and would not disappoint. Thus she found herself obliged to repeat her most successful paintings, although she did not enjoy this kind of work. It is not surprising, of course, that such repetitions seldom reach the quality of the first version. However, they offer an interesting insight into her method of work. She has painted the "Checkered House," for which there was a special demand, in various settings—winter, summer, spring, and fall. Originally the stopping-off station where the coaches changed horses, the red-and-white checkered house had become a landmark for the neighborhood. In her pictures it sometimes occupies the center of the scene, sometimes it is placed to one side; now the sky is sunny and blue, now cloudy and gray; in short, atmosphere and composition are different every time. Only by such variations, she said, had it been possible for her to go through with "those dreadful orders." And she has handled all other "repeat paintings" in a similar fashion.

By 1943 the rush for her pictures had become so overwhelming that the old lady became distressed at her inability to "keep up." She would have liked to paint new subjects, but could not get around to it, with so many demands for copies of the old ones. During one of my visits, we talked over the situation. After speaking in her quietly amused way about all those people who wanted the same pictures over and over again, she began to discuss the possibility of finding new subjects. She grew quite interested and earnestly considered various ideas. As soon as one seemed to make sense with her, she embraced it with youthful enthusiasm. Many people had wanted Thanksgiving pictures and she had always centered them around the theme of catching the turkey. How about showing the arrival of the guests, for a change? The idea clicked; one could see how her mind got busy on it and how the theme began to crystallize. A few weeks later she had completed the new picture. She had entered into the spirit of the new theme with whole-hearted freshness and pleasure.

She called the picture "Home for Thanksgiving." It shows a white clapboard house in front of which two—needless to say, old-fashioned—carriages have drawn up. The guests are about to alight; the hosts are coming out to greet them. Through an open door you can look into a kitchen, where a fire is merrily burning and the last preparations for the feast are going on. The house itself is depicted with special, loving care. Every last detail has been put in, to the dotted curtains behind the panes. A cold, bluish mountain panorama closes the November landscape. In this picture there is nothing of the routine that had begun to creep into her many repetitions of the old subjects.

Grandma Moses had never painted a Christmas picture, because interiors were not "in her line" and she felt that Christmas "belongs indoors." A casual remark about the preparations for Christmas beginning out-of-doors, about having to get the trees out of the woods before you can have them in the house, at once struck her imagination. Here was a new idea which she understood perfectly. Immediately she set to work on the picture. It is the one called "Out for the Christmas Trees": a wooded landscape in the deep of winter, with groups of people, busy hauling away trees. A man is carrying off a small one, another is taking away several on a sleigh. Nearby, children are skating and tobogganing. Five large birds in the sky give the picture a certain heavy grandeur unusual in her work.

[25]

Almost all of Grandma Moses' paintings are done on strong cardboard. She used canvas only at the very beginning, and twice again in 1943 and 1945. The size of her pictures rarely exceeds 24 by 30 inches. At first, they were much smaller, but then she settled upon this medium size which she likes best. She painted only two groups of large pictures after she had received several stretched canvasses 36 by 46 inches. One of the most interesting among them is "In the Park." After having acquired a certain practice in the handling of large spaces by repeating some of her older subjects on an enlarged scale, she permitted herself here a freedom of line and color which none of her small pictures possessed. In the foreground there is one of the covered bridges she often paints, and a bubbling stream rushing beneath it. On an embankment in front of the bridge, workers are having a picnic. To the left, a fallen tree spans the river. As we have noticed in others of her pictures, Grandma Moses composed this landscape somewhat like a stage setting: the middle part of the picture is framed by two tower-like structures, with roads winding up to them. A broadly painted mountain range forms the background. The clouds have been made with a dashing sweep of the brush. One comes to feel that the large space at her disposal prompted her to use a more daring technique. Her brush hurried along over the canvas, filling it with life and color. She no longer felt bound to put in every little detail, but painted the landscape in large bold strokes. Color has become a purpose in itself. The little figures almost disappear in the whole and seem to have been set in only to make the vastness of the scenery more impressive. And suddenly, amid all this newly found artistic freedom, there is a bit of "pure Grandma Moses": a tiny crimson plant, standing all by itself on a clearing near the right end of the bridge. It neither fits in with the rest of the picture, nor does it belong in this place. But there it is, to attract your attention, and it is like a little light in the dark forest.

It is hard to get Grandma Moses to speak about her actual painting. In her autobiography (pp. 37-45) she goes no farther than to explain how she prepares her panels. Only after long private conversations with her can one form a clearer idea of how she proceeds. It is vitally important to her that the panels be first covered with a layer of white paint. This gives the clear luminous quality to the colors which she later applies. When the surface has dried—she usually prepares several panels at a time—she starts by painting the sky. First she draws a thin pencil mark to fix "how far down it will reach." The wavy pencil outline also indicates the hills that will be painted below. And this is all the preliminary sketching she does. After the sky has been painted she draws the main objects with a few rough strokes: hills, houses, trees. But no details whatsoever—they are all put in with the paint-brush. This method explains why her pictures look so fresh and spontaneous, almost improvised. She plays with her theme and invents the details as she goes along, just as a child thinks up illustrations for a story he had heard.

It is amazing how many values Grandma Moses can achieve in a single color. Everyone who has seen her paintings recalls their multiple shades and tints of white and green. The shadings in her snow landscapes are especially elaborate. Foregrounds and backgrounds are treated differently. The snow has a darkish coloring in places where it has been walked on and sparkles in pure white where it has freshly fallen. In the distance it takes on various hues according to the light that falls upon it, and if a hedge or a path cuts across the white space, its coloring blends in with the light of that area. Sometimes such details are barely indicated, the lightness of the artist's touch reminding one of Japanese woodcuts. With her Spring landscapes she proceeds similarly. Here she varies the fresh green of the meadows. There is never a dull space. Every small area vibrates with life and color. Only through long and careful observation of nature can an artist render it with such love and deep understanding.

Grandma Moses' landscapes may be divided into four main groups which correspond to the four seasons. A definite color range prevails in each: white in the winter scenes, light green in the spring landscapes, a deep saturated green in the summer views, and brown in the autumn pictures. But there is abundant variation within these groupings; indeed, all her landscapes differ more or less from one another, even those dealing with the same matter. Asked how she manages to find so many new angles for one subject, Grandma Moses replied: "It is like looking out at the same landscape from various windows, it is the same landscape always, but it looks a little different every time."

After Grandma Moses completes a landscape, the figures must be put in. Questions about this aspect of her work have led to interesting conversations. She was asked why she often uses the same characters, varying them only in size and color. (Whereas we never come across two identical landscapes, we find the same groups in many of her pictures, especially in the "Sugaring-Off" and "Catching the Turkey" scenes.) She explained that the specific jobs depicted in "Sugaring-Off" are always done by the same people, and naturally they "have to look the same" in every picture, so that you may recognize at once what they are doing. There is the man who gathers the sap in his two buckets, and the man who brings in the wood and tends the fire to boil the sap, and the one who pours the wax; and there have always been and always will be children and young folks waiting to taste it. These remarks are very enlightening. They show her way of thinking to be the same that appears in children's drawings and in other primitive works of art. The figures constitute a sort of picture language intended to tell plainly what is taking place. The actions in "Sugaring-Off" are typical: they remain the same throughout the years, hence they must be represented in the same way every time.

The costumes of the men, women, and children, however, change. In some of Grandma Moses' pictures the figures wear the fashions of her youth, in others they are dressed in Eighteenth Century styles. The "Lookout" is a scene from the times of the Indian Wars, toward the end of the Eighteenth Century, the "Old Automobile" ran forty years ago, the "Fair" was a recent event. Naturally, Grandma Moses explains, the people have to be dressed in accordance with their time. In order to show that an action has taken place "way back in history," she must rely on models. She has a certain old book which she highly treasures, a combination of history and geography reader, and she consults its many illustrations whenever the necessity arises. She may "need a soldier," for instance, and so she looks for one in her book and paints him as she remembers the picture. She does not copy these figures, but obtains her inspiration from them.

"I have a look at the pictures of the book," she says, "and I see how they looked and how they acted. Then I try to paint the same way. It is also much simpler than if I had to invent them, and it saves time."

Yet, her figures always fit into their surroundings and never seem out of place—another proof of her artistic tact. Each of her pictures is a unit; landscape and figures are in perfect harmony.

Grandma Moses is interested in tradition and history. She is proud to trace her family centuries back. A number of her pictures tell about her forefathers, about Hezekiah King, who took part in the War of Independence, about Archibald Robertson, who built the first wagon to run on the Cambridge Pike. She depicts her own youth and shows herself as a little child. Strange events she has heard about long ago, like the Burning of Troy, or forest fires, which seem especially to impress her, turn up as subjects. But whether she represents idyllic farm scenes or historical events, her pictures always bear the imprint of her strong personality.

*

Grandma Moses' daughter-in-law Dorothy gives us a lively description of life on the Moses Farm. She says:

[29]

"When I married Hugh Moses, the youngest son of Thomas S. and Mary Robertson Moses, in April 1920, we made our home with my parents-in-law at their farm in Eaglebridge. Hugh continued operating the farm with his father, and since his father's death he has taken over the farm.

"As I knew nothing about living on a farm, I had lots to learn and 'Grandma' soon was gradually showing me how to make bread, pies, cakes, and canning in the summer. And in the winter time there was butchering, so I soon knew how to render lard, make headcheese, sausage, and can the meat. In the summer we would pick lots of berries, and Grandma really enjoyed doing this. Although I often wondered how she could stand it, she liked being out in the open, and seeing the cans filled and put away for winter. Carpet-weaving was also a hobby of Grandma's when I came here, and so I soon became quite fascinated with that and we spent many hours weaving. We did this work out in the shop—which in Revolutionary days was the original house and was called the 'house in the woods.'

"When my first baby, Edward, was born, Grandma helped me care for him and was quite happy to have the opportunity once more; and also when my daughters Jean and Marjorie were born. She enjoyed making things for them and they thought of her as their second mother, and called her 'Bonny'—but now it's 'Gram.'

"After a few years, Grandma found housework was too much for her. And so, while she was at her daughter's home in Bennington, she started making yarn pictures, which were very beautiful—as she designed her own pictures and they were done in lovely bright colors. They attracted much attention among those who saw them. She gave away many and also sold some. She also enjoyed embroidering pictures and made quite a few of these—which were done in floss in beautiful colors. Making quilts of all different patterns was another hobby of Grandma's,

[30]

and of these she made many, giving them to her children and grand-children.

"When her sister Celestia called on us one day and saw these pictures, she told her she should try to paint some—she 'knew' she could as long as she could make such beautiful ones in yarn. For her first picture Grandma used a piece of canvas which had been used for mending a threshing machine cover, and some old house paint. We told her it was very good and to try and paint more—which she did.

"When Grandma finishes a picture she always puts it out on display for my husband and me to see and to judge and to make any suggestions—which we very seldom have to do. We are the critics, she says, and we really enjoy and become more interested in her work.

"Some of the first she painted, Hugh and I took along with some yarn pictures down to the Woman's Exchange in Thomas' Drug Store in Hoosick Falls where they were put on display in the window. This is where the ball started rolling for Grandma. One day Louis Caldor, an art collector from New York, who was passing through Hoosick Falls, stopped at the drugstore and was very much amazed at the wonderful collection. He went in and asked all about the pictures and who the artist was and where she lived. Later he came here and met Grandma. He asked her to paint some pictures for him, which she did, and which he brought to New York, where her first exhibition took place at the St. Etienne Gallery. One of her first pictures which she said was a try-out she gave to the mail carrier as a Christmas gift. He was very much pleased.

"Grandma had never been to an exhibition until she went to her own exhibit at Gimbel's in New York in November 1940, a month after her one-man show at the St. Etienne Gallery. In May 1941, Hugh and I persuaded her that she should attend the exhibition held at the Syracuse Museum of Fine Arts, where her picture "The Old Oaken Bucket" won first prize of $250. When her painting was brought out on the stage and it was made known it had won the prize given by Mr. Thomas J. Watson, there was a terrific applause, and everyone arose to honor Grandma, who graciously was asked to step upon the stage. Everyone just flocked around her and asked so many questions, one would think she was a movie celebrity. Everyone tried to shake hands with her or to ask her about her paintings, until finally we decided she was getting tired from so much attention and excitement—we almost had to carry her away from her many admirers.

"High school students often have used Grandma as their topic in school essays. A graduate from Cambridge High School based her essay on Grandma. Students in Albany, Stillwater, and Hoosick Falls also wrote about her, thus showing she is greatly admired by the very young together with the old who have talked about her on the radio. All this pleases her in a modest way. Grandma has always wanted to be busy, as she says: 'Idle hands make mischief.'

"Grandma paints in her room upstairs in the east side. It is a large room with two windows which let in plenty of sun and air. As you enter the room your eyes immediately look across the room to Grandma sitting in a straight chair, maybe on a couple of books, one a catalogue of Sears or Montgomery Ward, where she orders so many of her brushes and tubes of paint, the other a very ancient Latin Bible, which was formerly used as door-stop around the house. These make her higher, to paint more easily her pictures which are in front of her on a very old pine table. The light from one window comes over her left shoulder.

"Grandma has her picture she is painting, on an old mixing board covered with newspaper, and this is on the table. Then she doesn't get any paint on her table. She has about thirty tubes of paint laid out, all colors in front of her, also metal jar covers with different colors mixed in them—one cover has a little turpentine to clean off brushes. There are several different-size paint brushes laid out. Then on the table are a couple of quart cans of white paint and a large brush which are used in

[32]

painting over her canvasses before she is ready for her pictures. At one end of the table is a box holding small nails, used to secure pictures in frames, a large blue pencil for addressing the crates of pictures when sent to the galleries. Then on the table is an old white cup with turpentine and a piece of white cloth in it, to use to wipe up any paint which might get on something. Also there may be an apple, orange, dish of candy, or some crackers, peanuts, potato chips, cookies, or popcorn, a cup of tea or coffee, which she lunches on when so busy. (The box compartment of this table in olden times was used as a place to keep their pewter dishes, and bread.) Over the table is a wall light with a 150-watt bulb which enables Grandma to paint at all times of the day and on the darkest of days in the winter. Under the light are letters, containing orders for pictures, pinned on the wall. These are also pinned on the wall back of Grandma, on the side of her dresser. Across from Grandma on the same side of the room is the other window, and in front of it are several plants which she enjoys taking care of. Along the side of the room there are canvasses painted white, waiting to have a picture painted on them, pictures partly done or all done, and also frames waiting to be tacked in and finished up. Side of her bed is an antique cherry stand with a small radio on it. Also a reading lamp, so she can read if she likes. She enjoys the radio when working, or sometimes when she retires she listens to a good program.

"She often plans a picture while resting or when she can't sleep. One time, when she was ill in bed and very discontented to stay there, as she said she should be doing something, and being confined to her bed with grippe was an idle waste of time—so when I was in the room caring for her, she said she had decided to paint the picture 'The Old Oaken Bucket,' which was the first picture she painted as soon as she got up around and was able to paint. And in a couple of months it was the prize-winning picture at the exhibition in Syracuse, in May 1941."

[33]

It is hard to tell exactly how many pictures Grandma Moses has painted since she was discovered eight years ago. She worked long over some of them, others, especially repetitions, were quickly completed. She once said that in such instances she works on several pictures at a time, lining them up in a row and doing first the sky, then the clouds, and so on. She treats new subjects more elaborately, of course, trying out her colors and often toning down a harsh red or blue to make it blend with the atmosphere of the picture.

Soon after her first exhibition Grandma Moses' brother provided her with small printed labels to be pasted on the back of her pictures. They bear the artist's portrait and the inscription:

> Anna Mary Robertson Moses,
> Eagle Bridge, N. Y.
> Born Sept. 7, 1860.
> Date of painting . . . . . .
> No. of painting . . . .
> Title . . . .

She now places these labels on the backs of all her pictures. But in spite of this impressive "bookkeeping," the information given on the labels is not always correct. Some numbers occur twice, other series are omitted altogether. The old lady now and then seems to lose track of them. The dating too is sometimes inaccurate: many pictures bear the same date. Perhaps this is to be explained by the fact that Grandma Moses had set herself certain days of delivery on which she dispatched several pictures at the same time to her customers. An entire group of paintings, regardless of when they had been actually completed, thus received the same date. But it also happened that she dated certain pictures several months ahead.

An introduction to the paintings of Grandma Moses would be incomplete without a few words about the personality of the artist. She is a very intelligent woman who makes a strong impression on everybody who meets her. She has most definite ideas and opinions of her own; she goes her own way and is not easily ruffled by anything. She is slight and very lively, always active, in spite of her years. She has a wonderful sense of humor, and can speak about the shortcomings of her fellow men with a twinkle in her eye. But she is never sarcastic. Her kind and good-natured approach to everything that surrounds her can be felt in her personal presence as well as in her work. If she knows one well, she enjoys telling little stories, mostly memories of when she was young, of the days she evokes in many of her pictures.

It was suggested to her some time ago that she write down her memories, and she promised to try. Almost a year elapsed, and then suddenly she sent two versions, both written entirely in her own hand. It seems that she had been in doubt as to what to describe. Her life had been a long one, many things had happened. The first version is chiefly concerned with her family history; she speaks about her parentage and tells what she knows about her ancestors. In the second version she discusses her own life, her husband and her children. But she winds up both sketches without touching upon the subject of her painting. Urged to include this latter part of her life, she sent a third, more comprehensive, version in which she begins by repeating most of what she had said in the two previous ones, and then goes on to speak about the last years which, though they made her famous, had not before seemed important enough to her even to mention them.

In editing Grandma Moses' autobiography, I have eliminated the repetitions, but all the facts have been retained, needless to say, as well as the old lady's personal way of spelling.

A letter, accompanying her biography, characterizes Grandma Moses' modesty. She writes: ". . . Here is my lifes History, can you make any thing out of it, is there any thing that I have not told you, if so, let me know. You see, I don't know how to go about these things."

In this book Grandma Moses speaks in her simple words and through her untaught pictures. Hers is a small voice in the great chorus of America, yet it is clear and true, and it is lifted in praise of life and of enduring, humble beauty.

May 1946   OTTO KALLIR

MY LIFE'S HISTORY

My Life's History
by Grandma Moses

I anna mary Robertson, was born back in the green meadows and wild woods, on a Farm in washington Co, In the year of 1860, Sept. 7, of Scotch Irish Paternal ancestry.

My ancestors came to this country at different times between 1740 and 1830, all of them settling in the immediate vicinity of southern washington county, new york State.

Here I spent the first ten years of my life with mother, Father and Sisters and Brothers.

Those were my happy days, free from care or worry, helping mother, rocking Sisters credle, taking sewing lessons from mother sporting with my Brothers, making rafts to float over the mill pond,

Roam the wild woods gathering Flowers, and building air castles.

I was one of a family of ten, my mother was one of eleven, my grandfather of fifteen, while my Husband was one of a family of twelve children.

My ancestors were early settlers in Cambridge.

My Grand Fathers Father came from Scotland, and his name there was Shonon. His Grand Father Joseph Shonan and son John Shonan went to the Isle of man as fishermen.

It is a small Island between Irland and England.

They lived with two Brothers by the name of Roch and a sister anastasia Roach.

after a time John Shanon and anastasia fell in love and wanted to get married. But as there was no Priest or minister on the Island, they had to cross over to Irland,

[39]

they gave the Priest their names, and He said there was no such name in all Irland.

and He named them John and anastia Shanahan.

now, if there is any property in Scotland we could not clame it, as the name has been changed.

I always disliked the name, and still dislike it. Probably it was costumery to put *han* on all of Irish names, as they do *van* on all Dutch names, I don't know.

John and Anastia had four or five children, my Grand Father Gregory Shanahan, the eldest child remembered when a little child, of siting on the floor and playing with his Grandpa Shonon silver buckles on his slippers.

He must of died when my Grand Father was qwite small, as He did not remember him so well.

My Grandpa parants boath died when Granpa was eleaven years old with fever. leving Grandpa the oldest to care for his Sister and two or three Brothers. as they had no kin there,

He found Homes for them with the help of the neighbors.

Then one of the neighbors gave Him a lofe of Bread, and in the daun of morning, He started acrost the country to find an uncle.

His mothers Brother, James Roch.

He walked all day, and just before sundown He came to his uncles Home, But the uncle was dead. and the widow sat on a plow, and was weeping hard, with her three or four little children around her.

He told her who he was, and that he would plow while she went to the House and got some thing to eat.

She had borrowed the Horse for the day to plow her garden, but so week that she could not hold the plow but for a short time.

and the garden was but half done. Grandpa plowed till dark, then took the Horse Home.

[40]

But the neighbor told Him to come get the Horse and finish the garden for his aunt.

He lived with her and helped to care for her children till they could do for themselves.

Probly about fiftween years.

When He came to this country, about the year 1836 or 8 as neer as I can tell.

He came from country Ross Waxford Irland, with his Brother Silverster,

Coming over on the same Ship that Grandma and her Brothers Peter and John, and a Sister Margret Devereaux were on.

John Devereaux was a Salor and payed thir passage.

The capton of the Ship was a cousin by marrige to Grandma Shanahan, Capton archibald Buchanan a Scothman. He had sailed in meny waters.

Grandpa and Grandma meet on board ship first.

then after reaching america they boath went to woork,

Grandma woorked for a famaly in waterford till she was married.

My Grandma Shanahan, was Bridget Devereaux, She was left an orphan in early girlhood, with a Sister and three Brothers,

The Sisters were taking by a aunt, Bridget Senet, mother in law to capton Beaucanon.

mrs. Senet keep a store and the girls were a great help to her. For some time my Grandmas duty was to go doun stairs in the morning, and take doun the shutters and dust up the store.

The aunt had a very talkitine Parrot,

there was a very poor famaly across the cort from the store, and sometimes, they did not have anything to eat,

Grandma would sneak a loft of Bread under her apron for them.

one day the Parrot told on her. then her aunt forbid her to take any more Bread,

[41]

now here is something more of Grandpa life,

when He came to this country, He woorked in Pitstoun, n.y. for some time for 50 c. a day. But He saved up enough to buy himself a comfortable Home where He lived and died, about 1877. I think, He had a fairly good education for his day.

He went to night school in Irland while living with his aunt,

He also had learned the shuemakers trade, so that he made all of his Children shoes.

I have seen him on woork on them.

my mother has said that she was twelve years old before she had a pair of boughten shoes.

mother comanced to go to school in the winter she was seven years old.

She left when eleven years old.

now this has been to give you insight in to my four Fathers (!) familys.

my Great Grand Father Hezekiah King was born in amenia Dutchess county n.y. 1755.

He was the son of capt John King and Elizabeth Fenner King.

Hezekiah King rade his Horse in to the valley before the Revolution war in which he served.

He taught school in that toun and, there cleared land and built him a Home about 1786,

Hezekiah King enlisted in the albany county militia and marched to meet the British.

He served at ticonderoga, and his poudar horn is still there and bears this inscription.

Hezekiah King. ticonderoga. Feb. 24th 1777.

Steal not this horn for fear of shame.

for on it is the owners name.

Hezekiah King olest Daughter was my Grandmother on my Fathers side.

my Fathers GrandFather was archibald Robertson, born in Scotland in 1748.

came to this country, coming to the Cambridge valley, and located on the hills west of Coily.

He was a wagon maker by trade he built the first wagon that ever ran over the cambridge pike,

Building it with an ax and saw. in later years he made the best wagons, between Boston and Buffalo, a Presbyteren by creed; some what of a musician, and a believer in second sight.

His oldest son was my Grand Father, william archibald Robertson,

my Father Russell King Robertson. a Farmer and inventor, a beleaver in beauty and refindment.

From the Kings I got art, from the Robertsons inventive faculty, from the Shanahans thrift, the Deveraux generousity.

*

Now, to go on about myself:

In 1870 began the hard years, Schooling was in those days in the country three months in summer, three in winter, little girls did not go to school much in winter, owing to the cold, and not warm enough clothing, there for my School days were limited,

alltho I was kept busy helping at Home, and the neighbors,

when twelve years of age I left Home to earn my own living as then was called a hired girl,

This was a grand education for me, in cooking, House Keeping, in moralizeing and mingleing with the out side world,

I went to live with a Family by the name of mrs. and mr. Thomas whitesides, they were lovely people, while well along in years,

I was cared for by them as a child of thair one,

[43]

Presbyterians by creed,

one of my duties was to drive the Horse "old black joe" to church for them on Sunday mornings, and place boquets on the Pulpit in the church and always remember the text,

living with the whitesides for three years, careing for mrs. whiteside who was an invalid and died,

Then I kept house for mr. whiteside for a year till his nephue and wife could come and take care of the Farm, and Him,

I was very proud in those days, could get up such fine dinners for his Friends who came from far off to see him,

when the Minster came and I could bring out the fine linen and the china tea set, and the heavy Silver, then with hot bisqwits home made butter and Haney, with Home cured dryed beef, I was proud,

But I some times now, think they came for eats more than to see Him,

Then mr. whiteside died,

and I drifted away from that neighborhood.

*

In 1880, still working as a hired girl, and careing for the sick, Those were busy days,

In the Fall of 1887,

nov. 9, I married Thomas Solomon Moses, a Farmer by occupation, a Grand son of the famous Dr. Moses,

we left on our wedding trip for north carolina to take charge of a Horse ranch,

But we never reached thire,

we got as far as Staunton Virginia where we planned to stay over the weekend, and there we were kidnaped or I should say over perswaded, to go no father south and to settle in the middle of the Shenandoah Valley,

[44]

So we hired a Farm near Staunton verginia for a year to see if we would like the south,

and the people there were over anxious for northeners or wessners to come in and build up the State,

They were in a way helpless since the colared help had been taking from them,

We remained on this Farm one year, then moved farther doun the Valley on to a Six hundred acre dairy Farm,

Here I commenced to make Butter in pound prints and ship it to the white Sulphur Springs, w, va,

I also made potato chips, which was a novelty in tho days, this we continued for sevarel years,

Here our ten children were Born,

And there I left five little graves in that beautiful Shenadoah Valley,

Coming to new york State Dec. 15, 1905, with our five children to educate and put on thire one footing,

we bought a Farm and went in to the dairy business selling milk, and doing genarel Farm woork,

Here my oldest daughter married and left Home, Here my two oldest sons bought a Farm and struck out for them selves,

Here Jan 15, 1927, my Husband died, my youngest son and wife taking over the Farm,

I live now with my youngest son who cares for the Farm,

I have four children living, eleven Grandchildren, and four Great-Grandchildren,

*

When I was quite small my Father would get me and my Brothers white paper by the sheet, it was used in those days for newspapers, He liked to see us draw pictures, it was a pennie a sheet and it lasted longer than candy, my oldest Brother loved to draw Steam Engines, that was a hobby with Him, the next Brother went in for animals, But as for myself I had to have pictures and the gayer the better, I would draw the picture, then color it with grape juice or berries any thing that was red and pretty in my way of thinking. Once I was given some carpenters red and blue chalk,

Then I was rich,

But children did not have so much in those days, we appreciated what we did get,

Then came the days when I dabbled in oil paint and made my lamb scapes as my Brothers said I called them, they had some brilliant sun sets, and Father would say "Oh not so bad"

But mother was more practical, thought that I could spend my time other ways,

Then in school teacher would give us maps to draw, and I would make the mountains in my one way, the teacher liked them, and would ask if he might keep them,

Then long years went by, one days my Daughter asked me to make her a worsted picture, She had seen one and liked it, and thought I could do one better, well I tryed it and it was a success, so, as I could handle a large needle, and wosted, I made meny a picture, and gave away meny of these, then my hands were geting tired and lame so that I could not sew as I had allwise,

my Sister suggested why not try oil paints, so I did, sending some to the Ladys exchange.

I exhibited a few at the cambridge Fair with some cand fruits and Rasberry jam,

I won a prize for my fruit and jam. but no pictures.

one day a mr. Luis Caldor an engineer and art collector passing through the toun, saw and bought four of my paintings. a short time after this three of these found thir way into the museum of modern art exhibition in n.y. city.

Mr. luis Caldor first discovered my art that led to fame, and to Him I'm very thankfull.

Mr. Caldor insisted on taking some of the pictures down to new york to show in the Galleries,

I had the first exhibit of my paintings placed in the Gallerie St. Etienne, 46 west 57 street,

when my exhibition opened large number of elderly people came having heard my story,

In the year 1940, I spoke to 400, people at the thanksgiven forum in Gimbels auditorium

again in 1941. I won a n.y. state art prize for a painting called "the old oaken Bucket",

Some one has asked how I paint and what on.

well I like masonite tempered presd wood. the harder the better,

I prefer it to canvas, as it will last longer,

I go over this with linseed oil, then with three coats of flat white paint, now I saw it to fit the Frames.

A picture with out a fraim is like a woman with out a dress. In my way of thinking.

Now this is to give you an idea of who and what I am.

GENEALOGICAL NOTE

ARCHIBALD ROBERTSON: Came from Scotland with brother William, between 1750 and 1770; settled temporarily in Massachusetts; left brothers John and Alexander in Scotland; sailed from Glasgow. Archibald built himself a cabin in Washington Co., N. Y. Several Robertsons came from Scotland, and settled in Washington Co., particularly near Cambridge and Argyle. Archibald spent his winters teaching school in New England and his summers on his farm. Married Martha Selfridge (died March, 1795). Married (2) Rebecca Carswell (died November, 1799). Married (3) Elizabeth Bishop. He died June 18th, 1814, age 66.

He had 7 children by first, 2 by second, 6 by third marriage. Children: William, Alexander L., Oliver (died 1794), Martha, Amy, Joel, John A., Archibald, Asa, Zenas, Alvan, Martha, Ebenezer, Abner C., Rebecca.

William Alexander: Born Cambridge, N. Y., May 4, 1783. Died August 1, 1838, near Blandon, O. Married January 1804, Sarah King (daughter of Hezekiah King, born May 23, 1786).

Children all born Cambridge, N. Y.: Hezekiah, Archibald, Elzia Shepard, William King, Ruhama.

Russell King: Born May 23, 1820, died June 12, 1909. Married September 25, 1856, Margaret Shannahan (Born January 20, 1840, died February 24, 1909).

Children: William Laster, Horace Greeley, Anna Mary, Arthur Marion, Celestia, Amy, Winona Grace, Jasper Devereux, Sarah, Frederick Eugene.

Anna Mary: Born September 7, 1860. Married Thomas Moses. Residing Eagle Bridge, N. Y.

Children: Winona R., Lloyd, Forrest, Anna May, Hugh.

—From *Robertson Family Records*, by J. Montgomery Seaver.
(American Historical-Genealogical Society, Philadelphia, 1928.)

THE PLATES

Plate 1

SUGARING-OFF

In the maple orchards long ago,
after the maple sap had been
evaporated till it would spin a
hair, then a call was sent out
to all of the young people to
come to the waxen,
  they would pour the thick
syrup on dishes of snow for
each to eat,
    they would eat their fill
and go home to dream sweet dreams,

Plate 2

THE OLD OAKEN BUCKET

Situated in the town of Cambridge.
Washington Co. N.Y. Back in the year
of 1760, this was the child Hood Home.
of Paul Dinnis,
I have been asked. why I panted the
old oaken Bucket, I have painted a
good meny of them, and I wish now
that I had sent the History, with them,
It would of been a monument to that
poor forgoten Boy Paul Dinnis.
mrs David Burch, an old Lady. and I were
geting a drink of water at a well, and
she said, do you Know whate well
you are drinking from,
no I did not Know,
Then she told me that was the well
of the old oaken Bucket,
and went on telling me the History.
How when a very little girl her Great
Great Grand Father took her by the
hand, and lead her acrost the Bridge
where the cateract fell, But she never
remembered of coming back,

said that her G. Grate Grandpa Had a
cloak on his shoulders, and a gun in
his hand, and he was agointo husk
corn beyound the pond,

and when they got there her G. Grand
pa spread his cloak on the ground
for her to play on while He husked
corn,

why she was with Him she did not
Know,

there might of been a funeral or a
wedding in the neighborhood,

while G. Grandpa was busy husking
a large Bear came down from the wild
woods, and comenced to eat the husked
corn.

she creep up under her G. Grandpa
arm, and he told her not to be afriad,
the Bear would eat what he wanted and
then go away, she remembered of
seing the big ugly Bear going back
to the woods,

she told me that her G. Grandpa
oldest Brother Paul Dennis liked one
of the neighbors Dawchters and her

Father thought Paul not good enough
for her, and that made trouble,
So Paul left the country, and went
off to be a Sailor,
In those days it took three years to
become a Sailor,
and He was quite young, and very
Home sick, it was then He wrote
those verses. of the old oaking Bucket,
when returning to Boston, after
three years. He gave the verses to
one woodworth who set them
to music, and there for claimed
them as His composing,
this was told to me 70 years ago,

Plate 3

THE CHECKERED HOUSE

the Checkered House is old,
this as it looked in 1853,
It was the Headquarters of
General Baum in the revolution
war, and afterwards He used
it as a Hospital,
then it was a stoping place
for the stage,
where they changed Horses every
two miles,
oh we traveled fast in those
days,

Plate 4

BRINGING IN THE CHRISTMAS TREE

---

oh with what joy, and pleasure
as we get to geather, to go for the
christmass tree
   what aircastles we build as
we slide down the Hill
   oh who can rebuild what
we see on that christmass tree,

Plate 5

GRANDMA GOES TO THE CITY

this was a request for
Grandma moses to go to the
Big city, new york.
    Grandma who had never
travled much,
what anticipation, and vexation
what commotion and confusion,
at last she is on her way.

Plate 6

EARLY SPRINGTIME ON THE FARM

there are the damp snow dayes,
when we love to go to the woods.
and look for the first bloom of the
trailing arbutus, which sometimes
blooms beneeth the snow,
   or geather the pussy willow.
those are the days of childhood,

Plate 7

BRINGING IN THE MAPLE SUGAR

---

this is one of my first paintings,
of bringing in the maple sugar.

Plate 8

SHENANDOAH VALLEY

this is a ~~scene where~~
Shanandoah River intersetes the
Blue Ridge mountains at the foot
of Boliver Heights,

Plate 9

CAMBRIDGE

Part of cambridge valley lies in the
teritory granted in 1688 by Gov thomas
Dangan,
the toun was Born in 1773,
Hezekiah King rode his hors in to the
valley before the Revolution war
in which served,
He taught the first school in
cambridge,
Farther north six years before
the Revolution, John weir had
cleard land and built him a Home,
and near by was the Green settlement.
they were the first settlements in
the toun,
cambridge lies betwen the north
line of the Hoosick Patent and
Stevensons corners, now coila,
at the Time the toun was founded,
cambridge was a part of albany, Co,
and covered all the territory now
Known as white creek and Jackson,
two beautifull valleys,
archibald Robertson came to
cambridge valley about 1770, and
located on the hills west of coila,—

a wagon maker by trade,
    John Robertson was on the
high seas, with his two Daughters
and three sons, when war was
declared between England and
america,
    He settled neer Coila, and
built the first good House that
was built in Cambridge,
    It is still standing there a
two story House,
    as He did not Know what
the quarrel was about He could'ent
deside with either,
    there for He was branded a tory,
They made it so hot for Him,
He went to Canada, with His two
Sons, and started a mill and a
    nursery,
    Leaving His two Daughters to care
for the Home till He could get back,
    the Daughters were girls in their
teens,
one night they sat busy spinning,
and the Boys of the neighborhood
thought to make them trouble,
Shot through a window and
set thir distaff on thir spinning wheel afire,
    This so frighten the girls that
they put out the fire, and blew
out their candles, and hid beneath

the window sills, till nearly
morning, then they crept out
of the House locking the doors,
 crept under the shrubery
across the road up the Hill where
mary McClellan Hospital now
stands,
 There an old Scotch man lived,
they went to ask advice from
Him,
 He took them in to his family,
and would not let them go back
till He could go with them,
 when they did go back they
found the House had been robbed,
of meny things,
among them they had two large
chestes filled with nice bedding
that had been thir mothers, and
they had brought it from Scotland
 In time they found one of
the chests but no bedding,
 mr. culvor kept the girls with
His family untill the Father could
come back,
 In those days they went mostly an
horse back, with another horse as
beast of burden,
 in time the Daughters married,
and now their descendents are
scattered all over the town of
 cambridge,

Plate 10

SUGARING–OFF IN MAPLE ORCHARD

Londonderry setters back in
1800,   Had to depend on maple
sugar and Honey for all the
sweeting that they reppvired,
So early in the spring they
would get shoemack, to make
spiles, for the maples trees,
then they would chisel out
parts of logs for sap containers,
then in march tape the trees,
geather the sap evaporate it to
make what sugar they would
need for the year,

Plate 11

FIRE IN THE WOODS

This is emanation from that
old song,
Fire in the mountains run Boys run,
Fire in in the mountains fun Boys fun.

Plate 12

CAMBRIDGE VALLEY

This is a north west veiw of my
Fathers Russell King Robertson Farm,
on Oak Hill,

Looking south east you can see
Van Ness Hill, and Battle field Park.
the Owl Kill, and the state road,
runing from Troy to Glens Falls.

some call this a pretty valley.
But give me the Shandoah valley,
every time,

Plate 13

BLACK HORSES

I have been told that my Great Grand
Father E, Robertson, was sent out as a
look out, back in the year of 1777,

He was plowing a field in cambridge
near where now stands the mary
McClellan hospital,

when far to the west he saw a patch of
woods that seemed to change each
time he went around the field,

He watched it closely,
and made up his mind that it was
an army,

He unhitch his horses from the plow,
turning one loose, and rode the other down
through Coila, warning all that the British
were coming,

On his way to Bennington he met the
Bennington Boys coming, they had received
nuse that a army was coming up from
Troy to tate meny barrels of pork,

But they meet near Walloomsac and had
fierce battle there, and there one of
my Great Grand Fathers black horses was
Killed,

Plate 14

HOME OF HEZEKIAH KING

this was the Home of Hezekiah King built about the year of 1778, was distroyed in 1800, by fire.

It was a shingled House, the sils were Hued about 8 or 10 inches thick from twelve to twenty inches wide, the cellar walls still mark the site of the old Home.

Hezekiah King was born in amenia Dutches county, n.y. 1755, He died in cambridge, n.y. 1823. He was the son of capt John King, and Elizeabth Fenner King;

when he was about twenty years old He left his Home, and traveled into the cambridge valley looking for place in the wilderness, where He might build his future Home

In a few months his country was calling for soldiers,

He enlisted in the 16th albany county militia, and marched to meet the British, He served at Ticonderoga, there He carved his powder Horn.

Here in this valley He built a church, so it was called the King church valley,.

Plate 15

THE TRAPPERS (II)

I lived neer Greenwich wen I
was small,
    my Father Russell.King. Robertson,
had a Flax mill, and employed,
merry men,
    and they would do Hunting, and
traping between Times, making
quite a sum of money through
the winter

Plate 16

I onced was asked why they had covered
Bridges, well I think the covering was to protect
the timbers from Snow and rain,
so that they would not decay so fast,
as it was yute an undertaking to build a
Bridge across a rapid flowing stream.
But now they are swiftly passing away.
They were land marks in day's gone by.
There was the Hoosick Bridge, in early days
called the white House Bridge, the longest Bridge
in new york State, and now it is no more,
Eagle Bridge got it name from a large Eagle
that was nailed on one end of the Bridge,
Some years ago an Irishman coming to this
country looking for work, was sent to
Eaglebridge,
there was a man there who hired meny hands,
By the name of whitman gosland, and this
Irishman had forgoten the name of the man.
or place, He walked for miles asking people
if they could tell him where there was a man, that
would give him work, He dident recollect the name,
but it reminded Him of the whistland gosling, near
the Bridge with the Hawk on it, and meny call
it that to this day,.

Plate 17

OVER THE RIVER TO GRANDMA'S HOUSE

Over the river and through the wood,
Trot fast, my dapple-gray!
   Spring over the ground,
   Like a hunting-hound!
For this is thanksgiving day!

Over the river and through the wood,
and straight through the barn-yard gate,
   we seem to go
      Extremly slow.
It is so hard to wait!

Over the river and through the wood:
Now Grandmothers cap I spy!
   Hurrah for the fun!
   Is the pudding done?
Hurrah for the pumpkin-pie!

Over the river and through the wood.
To Grandfather's House we go
   The horse Knows the way
   To carry the sleigh
Through the white and drifted snow.

Over the river and through the wood,
oh, how the wind does blow:
   It stings the toes,
   and bites the nose.
as over the ground we go.

Over the river and through the wood.
to have a first rate play.
   Hear the bells ring
      Ting a ling-ding!
Hurrah for Thanksgiving Day!

Plate 18

OVER THE RIVER

This was my Grandmothers
Kings old Home,
and when thanksgiven came
we were all expected Home
to dinner,
there were meny young
people like our selves,
and we would have a grand
time in playing,
Sports of all kinds, as we were
of different ages, some old
some young,

Plate 19

CATCHING THE THANKSGIVING TURKEY

why do we think we must have
turkey for thankgiven.

just becaus our Forefathers did,
they had it becaus turkeys were
plentyfull, and they did not
have other Kinds of meat,

now we have abundance of other
Kinds of luxuries,

Poor Turkey, He has but one
life to give to his country,

Plate 20

MOUNT NEBO IN WINTER

while living in the Shanadoah valley in vergina our
Home was called mt nebo, and when we came back
to new york state the children wanted to call the new
Home mt nebo, they thought it very approbate,
and so it is, It was my Home in 1900, and still is. there
are meny changes, but still my Home.
the mail carryer gave it that name, He was thinking
of the Burial of moses,

MOSES.

Plate 21

McDONELL FARM

---

away back in 1840, the farms were large, and they had meny hired men, to till the land, as they raised nearly all of thir food, such as wheat, corn, oats, rhy and buckwheat and lots of lifestock, Horses, Cows, sheep, this called for woork, From the sheep, they spun the wool for yarn, to be woven into cloth for Blankets, and cloathing, They did ther own weaveing.

Thir sweets was obtained from the bees and the maple trees, in the spring of the year,
The Geese, turkeys, ducks, and Hens, were the womens care, there was allwise a plenty of food, But no idle hands, It could well be called. ^{mc}Donell Farm. with a yuck. yuck. here, ba. ba. there, and a cluck. cluck. every where, then would come the Harvest time, and the owener of the Farm, would get his men and scythes, togeather, and roll a barrel of whiskey into the medow, and the fun would begin, before noon every man would be laid out on a Haycock, drunk as a Lord, They thought whiskey Keep away malaria, and gave them strength, and energy, But after a harty dinner they were ready for woork again, they sow^{ed} thir flax, pulled and brok it, dress it, spun and wove it, in cloath, ^{and} fine linen,

Plate 22

IN THE PARK

---

meaning nearer God intentions, nearer to nature.
where in some respects, we are free.
where there is beauty and tranquillity,
where we some times long to be, quiet and
undisturbed, free from the hub bub of life,

Plate 23

IN THE SPRINGTIME

In the Spring time of life there is a plenty to do.

Plate 24

THE RED MILL

this is over the River to Grandpa
House where the mill ran all day
long
        where we children loved to go
But entrance was forbid you Know,

Plate 25

IN HARVEST TIME

they are sowing the seed of noble deed,
with a sleepless watch and an earnest heed.
with a ceaseless hand oer the earth they sow,
and the fields are whitening whereer they go
   Rich will the Harvest be,
Sown in darkness, or sown in light,
Sown in weakness or sowen in might,
Sown in meekness or sown in wrath.
   Sure will the harvest be,

Plate 26

HOOSICK FALLS IN WINTER

the Hill lands north of the
Hoosick. R. were the Hunting

grounds of the mohicans,
the Hoosick was thir River of
pines, and Schaghticoke was
thir minglin of waters,
Tioshoke was on the north side
of the Hoosick. R. at the place
where tree crossed the River.
(Tree Bridge) at Eagle Bridge where
the Owl Kill and Hoosick meet,
were the Indians corn fields,
Twelve acres at wallomsack was
thir paint mines,
Decayed iron ore,
Hoosick Falls. was called yweywich,
and was the Home of Cooper Leather
Stockings, some say Natty Bumfo
sleeps his last sleep in an unknown
grave in village limits,
the grant takes in the Fenner King.
Farm, also the south side of
Hezekiah King Farm,

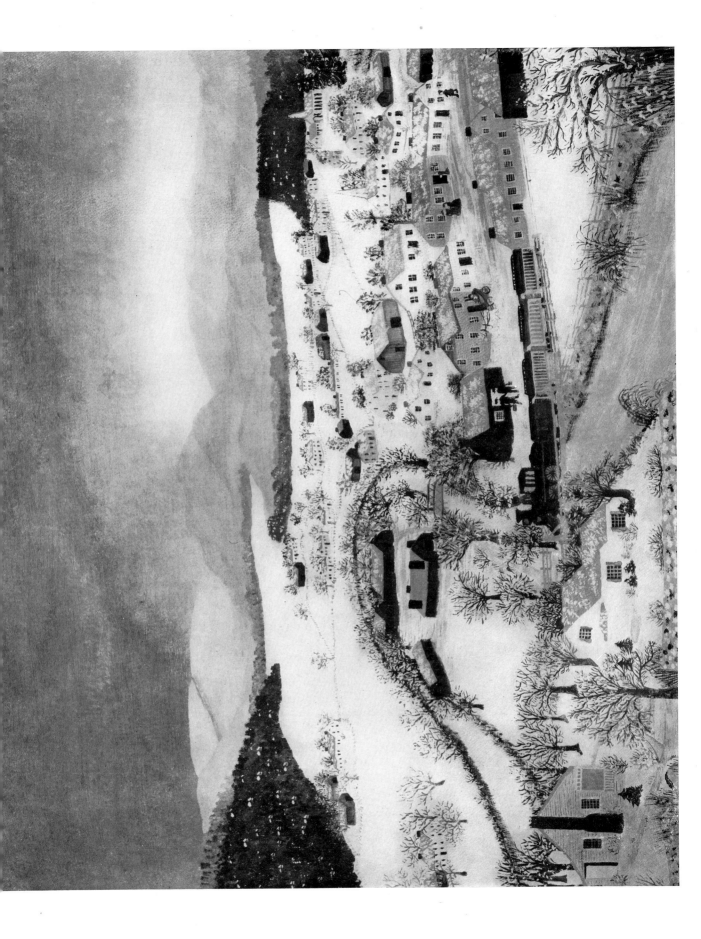

Plate 27

THE OLD AUTOMOBILE

the old automobile was a
nusance in it day,
But that like other things has
passed away,
    But some think now there
here to stay,
    But me thinks, that to will
pass some day,

Plate 28

HOME FOR THANKSGIVING

In some Homes this year will
be rejoicin, in others there
will be sorrow,
    But we that can give thanks
should,
    there is much to be thankfull for,
and praise, God for all blessings,
    and the aboundance of all things.

Plate 29

HAYING TIME

Haying time on the Farm,
is when you geather the
grain such as wheat oats
rye, hay, fruit, and berries of
all discription,
and the little folks geather
the eggs,

Plate 30

THE FIRST SKATING

this was a delightfull past
time in olden days for the
young people,
as for my self I was a one
foot skater,

Plate 31

PICNIC

the church picnic, was one
of the dayes that children
looked forward to through
the year,

then it was when they
could have all the cake and
lemonade they wanted,
water melon and peanuts was
a wonderfull treat,

Plate 32
THE LOOKOUT, 1777

the Lookout. 1777. vermont

In the early days of vermont and new york.
a look out was posted above the settlement to
sound a worning in time of trouble,
to call the men from wood and field
Here we see a Father telling his wife and children
to go back to the settlement as He has discovered
Indians,
the last indians of record in vermont. spent the
winter 1856, in a meadow neer Bellows Falls,
many of the early new England Homes, were equiped
with secret hiding closets, for the protection of
women and children during indian attacks,

Plate 33

MAY: MAKING SOAP, WASHING SHEEP

Back in the 1870. the Farmers
would allwise wash the sheep
after a few hot days before
sheering,
and the wifes would make
up the years supply of Hard an
soft soap, witch would be
a barrel or more, this was used
on wash day, and House cleaning.
we were thrifty in those days.
nothing wasted nothing lost,

Plate 34

A WINTER'S DAY

This is when zero stands at 25 or 30,
when we can not denye the pleasure of skating till we have bumped heads, and bleedy noses,
and the ice is like glass,

Plate 35

BONDSVILLE FAIR

this is a little Fair that is held up in vermont, one day in the year, when all of the natives come down from the mountain, in thir every day customs, the women in thir sun bonnets and check aprons, the men in patched overhauls, leading a cow or pig, the wimon with a few chickens, or braded rugs, may be an ox, and some beens.

they come to meet thir friends, and a day of pleasure, and they did say, if you were not drunk by ten oclock, they would put you in the coop and keep you there till you paid, a fine, that was thir way of making money.

a mean yankey trick, but they all wire had a large croud, and a joly good time,

Plate 36

GOING TO CHURCH

this was a pleasure in olden times to go to church, the man of the House would arise earloy, feed the stock, milk the cows, curry off the Horses, yoke up the oxen if in winter, to the long sleigh, placing there on a bundle or two of straw, white the wipe or mother, prepared a harty breakfast, and put up a good lunch, and helping to dress all old and young, in thir best, Banking up the fire in the fire place, for a warm room on thir return from church,

now the Father walks and drives the oxen, mother cuddles the little ones, and Grandma and Grandpa sits on the back of the sleigh and watches over the younger generation,

now we have reached the church, what an enjoyment here we can exchang the neus of the week, hear from the sick and the well, and spend the day in prayer, thankgiven and song, a day of pleasure and rest from drudgery.

If all was well in the neighborhood we would go Home singind those songs, "work for the night is coming", "sweet by and by," and this was a great favorate, "the mountains of Life",

and now the younger generation prefer to go to the movies.

Plate 37

WASH DAY

I painted this when I thought
over the verses that was in our
reading Book in school long ago.
oh monday was our washing day, and
while the clothes were drying a wind
came whistling through the line.
and set them all a flying.
I saw the shirts and petticots. go
flying off like witches,
I lost oh biterly I wept,
I lost my sunday breeches,
I saw them flying through the
are, alas to late to save them a
hole was in thir ample part,
as if an imp had wore them,

Plate 38

THE WHITESIDE CHURCH

This church was built by Phinehas whiteside, presbyterian by creed, it was built about the year 1800 as near as I can tell,

It was patronized by meny creeds. even the quakers.

It was built with wide pine planks running up and down,

It stood on the side of a hill by the side of a large track of woodland, the fields slopeing away from it down in to a valley where a stream of water flowed called the Fly Brook.

The church was largely attended, I have seen as meny as four hundred gather there for worship,

there were few churches in the community in those day's, and there being no other amusement the church and sunday school was very enticing for the younger generation, thus it went on for meny years. the Fathers and mothers would be laid to rest in the old burying ground, and a younger generation take their place, the church is still standing, and in good preservation,

Plate 39

OUR BARN

Our Barn.
this is the fall of the year, and there
are many odd jobs to attend to.
Feed to be stored away for the coming
cold weather.
the ground to be plow for rye. and
other crops before it is frozen hard.
Ditches to dig. Poultry to cull and house

Plate 40

CHRISTMAS EVE

this is christmass eve, and Grandma
has come from over the mountain to
help with the christmass tree.
and dinner for the coming day.
there will be rejoicing, and a good
time,

EXHIBITIONS OF PAINTINGS BY GRANDMA MOSES

(asterisk indicates one-man shows)

MUSEUM OF MODERN ART, N. Y. *"Contemporary Unknown Painters."* Private Members' Show, October 1939

*GALERIE ST. ETIENNE, N. Y. *First one-man show, October 1940*

*GIMBEL'S, N. Y. *November 1940*

*WHYTE GALLERY, WASHINGTON, D. C. *January 1941*

SYRACUSE MUSEUM, SYRACUSE, N. Y. *New York State Exhibition, May 1941*

GRAND CENTRAL GALLERY, N. Y. *June 1941*

*PINE CAMP, N. Y. *(Arranged by Munson-Williams-Proctor Institute, Utica, N. Y.) October 1942*

*AMERICAN-BRITISH ART CENTER, N. Y. *December 1942*

*BAR HARBOR, MAINE. *August 1943*

*CROCKER ART GALLERY, SACRAMENTO, CAL. *November 1943*

EVERHART MUSEUM, SCRANTON, PA. *August 1943*

UNIVERSITY OF NEW HAMPSHIRE, DURHAM, N. H. *November-December 1943*

*AMERICAN-BRITISH ART CENTER, N. Y. *December 1943*

INDIANA UNIVERSITY, BLOOMINGTON, IND. *January 1944*

*GALERIE ST. ETIENNE, N. Y. *February 1944*

*JAMES VIGEVENO GALLERIES, LOS ANGELES, CAL. *April 1944*

*MT. HOLYOKE COLLEGE, SOUTH HADLEY, MASS. *September 1944*

*SYRACUSE MUSEUM, SYRACUSE, N. Y. *October 1944*

*LAWRENCE ART MUSEUM, WILLIAMS COLLEGE, WILLIAMSTOWN, MASS. *October 1944*

ART ASSOCIATION OF RICHMOND, INDIANA. *October 1944*

METROPOLITAN MUSEUM OF ART, NEW YORK. *"Portrait of America,"* 1945-1946

*AMHERST COLLEGE, AMHERST, MASS. *November 1944*

GEORGE WALTER VINCENT SMITH GALLERY, SPRINGFIELD, MASS. *November 1944*

[135]

*GALERIE ST. ETIENNE, N. Y. *December 1944*

*CENTENNIAL CLUB, NASHVILLE, TENN. *February 1945*

NEBRASKA ART ASSOCIATION, LINCOLN, NEB. *March 1945*

*JAMES VIGEVENO GALLERIES, LOS ANGELES, CAL. *April 1945*

*CURRIER GALLERY OF ART, MANCHESTER, N. H. *May 1945*

*MAXWELL GALLERIES, SAN FRANCISCO, CAL. *May 1945*

CORNELL UNIVERSITY, ITHACA, N. Y. *"Festival of Contemporary American Art," June 1945*

*WHYTE GALLERY, WASHINGTON, D. C. *June 1945*

*MONTANA STATE NORMAL COLLEGE, DILLON, MONT. *August-September 1945*

*UTICA PUBLIC LIBRARY, UTICA, N.Y. *October 1945*

*JAMES VIGEVENO GALLERIES, LOS ANGELES, CAL. *October-November 1945*

*NORFOLK MUSEUM OF ARTS AND SCIENCES, NORFOLK, VA. *November 1945*

MADISON SQUARE GARDEN, N. Y. *"Twenty-second Annual Women's International Exposition," November 1945*

CARNEGIE INSTITUTE, PITTSBURGH, PA. *"Painting in the United States, 1945" and "Painting in the United States, 1946"*

*POMONA COLLEGE, CLAREMONT, CAL. *January 1946*

ACKNOWLEDGMENT

The editor wishes to express his thanks to the following museums and collectors whose paintings by Grandma Moses have been reproduced in this book:

Mrs. Renée C. Amory, Mrs. A. T. Baldwin, Lt. Anson Brooks, Mr. Louis J. Caldor, Miss Katharine Cornell, Mrs. Alden K. Sibley, Mrs. Raymond F. Evans, Mrs. J. Winton Gottlieb, Mr. Raymond Harper, Mr. Jack Kapp, Miss Dorothy Liebes, Mrs. W. H. Osborn, Phillips Memorial Gallery, Washington, D. C., Mr. Frederic Newlin Price, Museum of Art, Providence, Rhode Island, Mr. Thomas J. Watson.